ZERO WEDDINGS & A FUNERAL
and then a LOT more funerals

KU-471-250

HE'S DEAD?

I AM GROOT?

I'M FINE. WHY DO YOU ASK?

I AM GROOT.

THE ROOM-TRASHING? THAT'S UNRELATED. I'M FINE.

I AM GROOT?

NO. HARD NO. WHY WOULD WE GO TO SOME STUPID FUNERAL?

IT'S ALWAYS THE SAME STUPID SPEECH.

"HE WAS A KIND, CARING SOUL, BLAH BLAH BLAH, SUCH A TRAGIC LOSS, BLAH BLAH, HE WILL LIVE ON IN OUR SMILES AND SONGS."

CLANK

SO HE KICKED THE BUCKET, SO WHAT? I HAVEN'T TALKED TO HIM IN YEARS.

I DON'T EVEN REMEMBER WHAT...

...HE LOOKS LIKE...

OH, HEY THERE. I'M FRANKIE.

LATER.

YOU **FAKED** YOUR DEATH?

WELL, YOU KNOW WHAT THEY SAY...

...LIFE IS LIKE A BOWL OF CHERRIES. IF YOU OWE SOMEBODY TOO MUCH MONEY, FAKE YOUR DEATH AND BUY A WIG.

HA! CLASSIC FRANKIE! BAD AT METAPHORS, GREAT AT GRIFTS.

SO, WHATCHA BEEN UP TO?

NOT MUCH. WENT TO PRISON, BROKE OUT OF PRISON, SAVED THE KNOWN UNIVERSE A COUPLE OF TIMES.

I AM GROOT.

OH YEAH, LAST MONTH WE COMPLETELY CUT OUT SUGAR.

OH, HERE, LEMME GET THIS.

REALLY? AREN'T YOU IN A "FAKE-YOUR-OWN-FUNERAL" LEVEL OF DEBT???

WELL, I'M NOT PAYING FOR IT WITH MONEY...

C'MON, YOU GET TOO FAMOUS TO HAVE FUN? LET'S DO THE OL' "HOBO'S HELLO."

FRANKIE WAS A KIND, CARING SOUL...

SUCH A TRAGIC LOSS...

HE WILL LIVE ON IN OUR SMILES AND SONGS...

I AM GROOT.

AGAIN... WHAT???

EXCUSE ME, SIR. WHAT WAS YOUR RELATIONSHIP WITH THE DECEASED?

HOW'D YOU FEEL ABOUT HIM DYING?

WHAT?! HE WAS JUST SOME GUY I KNEW! YOU WANT ME TO MAKE SOME BIG SPEECH?

I GOT NOTHING TO SAY. WHY'S EVERYONE MAKING A FEDERAL CASE OUT OF THIS?!

WELL, YOU'RE THE MAIN SUSPECT IN HIS MURDER.

OH.

CRAP.

WE'VE GOT FIVE WITNESSES WHO SAW YOU PUSH HIM OFF A MOVING TRAIN.

IT WAS AN ACCIDENT!

I AM GROOT.

I KNOW YOU'RE GROOT.

I DIDN'T MEAN TO-- FRANKIE?!

LOOK! OFFICERS! BEHIND YOU!

HA! YOU REALLY THINK WE'RE GONNA FALL FOR THE "HOBO'S HELLO"?

ALL RIGHT, FINE. PLAN B.

WHYTH BRORB TH RICHH SLUGG?* WHENTH YOUTH CANTH TRICKTH TWOOTH DUMMIESTH TO DOOTH IT FOR YOOTH.**

*They found Frankie's teeth at the crime scene, remember? He pulled them out!

**So. Okay. Basically, he said that he tricked them into breaking into the Slug's vault for him.

JSTH SIHTT TIGHT, SO I CNNTH GETH YR BONNNTHY.*

*Now, he's gonna turn them in and collect the bounty on their heads! Whoa! Stakes raised!

I AM GROOT!

FRANKIE... YOU...YOU...

YESTH? SOMETHINGTH YOO WANNA STHAY?*

*That one seems pretty clear. Am I over-explaining stuff?

I LOVE YOU.

...WAHTH?

I AM GROOT?

BECAUSE THERE'S ONLY ONE PERSON WHO'D NEED THAT MUCH BABY POWDER. AND THERE'S A *HUGE* BOUNTY ON HIS HEAD.

HIS NAME IS--

I AM GROOT?

I AM GROOT??

I'LL GET TO THAT. HIS NAME--

I'LL GET TO WHY HE NEEDS THE BABY POWDER! LET ME TELL THE STORY!

HI. I'M A LOSER.

"HIS NAME'S CHAMMY. HE'S A LOW-LEVEL LOSER SPACE SMUGGLER FROM SOME NOSELESS ALIEN RACE."

"HE WAS ONE OF THE FIRST BOUNTIES I EVER TRIED TO COLLECT.

"SO YOUNG ME CATCHES HIM IN A DESERT..."

FREEZE, SUCKA!

"...OR MAYBE IT WAS UNDER-WATER? I FORGET..."

FREEZE, SUCKA!

AFTER AN EPIC BATTLE, I THROW HIM IN THE BRIG AND FLY HIM TO--

I AM GROOT?

I'M GETTING TO IT! ANYHOW--

WHY DID YOU GO INTO SO MUCH DETAIL ABOUT YOUR MUSCLES?

MIND YOUR BUSINESS. *ANYHOW...*

"WHEN I GO TO GET CHAMMY OUT OF THE BRIG...

"HE'S GONE!

"THE CELL'S EMPTY. NO TRACE OF ANYTHING BUT A PUDDLE OF WATER.

"IT WAS SUPER EMBARRASSING."

NOW, WHERE WAS I? OH, RIGHT...

SO, I USED TO BE LIKE YOU. JUST A REGULAR COMIC BOOK READER.

THEN ONE DAY I WAS A CHARACTER.

SKREEEEEE

AND COMIC BOOK CHARACTERS THAT AREN'T HEROES... DON'T DO TOO WELL.

SO I POPPED OFF MY PANTS AND POPPED ON A MASK. NOW I'M A HERO!

ISN'T THERE MORE YOU HAVE TO DO?!

HONESTLY, NOT REALLY.

CRUNK!

THE BEST PART OF THIS COMIC BOOK UNIVERSE, ASIDE FROM THE NOT-EVER-HAVING-ANY-CELLULITE-EVER PART...

...IS THAT IT'S DESIGNED FOR HEROES! LIKE ME! FOR EXAMPLE...

SEE! DIDN'T DIE!

WUMP

THIS PROBABLY KILLS A CAR RIGHT?

STABBY STAB-STABS

SHOOTY SHOOT SHOOT

AND I BET THESE BULLETS HIT SOMETHING CONVENIENT AND VILLAINOUS!

CRAW

FWIP

FWIP

FWIP

DID THEY? IT'S COOLER IF I DON'T LOOK.

SPLAT

KRUNCH

IT'S NOT A *LOT* BETTER THAN NOT HAVING CELLULITE, BUT IT'S STILL PRETTY COOL.

FREEZE, SUCKA!

YOU DIDN'T GET THE TALCUM POWDER? WHAT HAPPENED?! WAS IT *REEVE*?

NO, NO. IT WAS-- DON'T WORRY ABOUT IT. BUT I NEED TO FIND ANOTHER WAY OFF THE PLANET!

OR A SHIP THAT'S POWERED BY SOMETHING LESS *RIDICULOUS*!

ALL RIGHT, I'LL SEE WHAT I CAN WORK OUT. HAVE YOU TOLD RUTH YET?

NOT YET. BUT SHE DEFINITELY KNOWS SOMETHING'S UP.

WE'VE BEEN FIGHTING.

MMM, WELL, EARTH WOMEN ARE DIFFICULT. DID YOU APOLOGIZE AND LET HER KNOW THAT YOU HEAR HER?

LIKE TEN TIMES! I MUST BE DOING IT WRONG BECAUSE IT'S ONLY MAKING HER ANGRIER.

WELL, THAT'S ALL I GOT. MAYBE *BUY HER SOME-THING*?

KRUNK

KRAK

"AND THEN I FINISHED THEM OFF WITH THIS AWESOME SPLIT KICK..."

...AND TOTALLY SAVED THE DAY. IT WAS AWESOME, CAROL.

WHY DID YOU GO INTO SO MUCH DETAIL ABOUT YOUR MUSCLES? I KNOW THAT'S NOT WHAT YOU LOOK LIKE.

WELL, I JUST WANTED TO PAINT A FULL PICTURE--

WHATEVER. CONGRATS ON STOPPING THE SUPER-DANGEROUS BABY POWDER THIEF.

NOW GET BACK TO NEW YORK, WE'RE SWAMPED!

OH. WELL, ACTUALLY, CAROL, WE WERE HOPING TO STICK AROUND.

WE'VE NEVER SEEN THIS PART OF THE COUNTRY AND--

SO YOU WEREN'T ABLE TO DO YOUR SECRET SELF-SERVING PLAN YET?

THERE'S NO SECRET SELF-SERVING--

LOOK, HEAD BACK NOW OR BECOME SOMETHING I DEAL WITH PERSONALLY!

--PSKHHH-- BREAKING UP--CAN'T HEAR--PSSKHH-- BATTERY DYING--SKRR.

ROCKET. THESE COMMUNICATORS ARE POWERED BY MINI-ARC REACTORS...

KRUNCH

...THEY DON'T RUN OUT OF BATTERI--

ALL RIGHT. I DON'T THINK SHE'S ONTO US, BUT WE GOTTA FIND CHAMMY FAST.

...NOW YOU'VE TOLD ME *EVERY-THING.*

NEXT STOP... *EARTH.*

OH! SQUIRREL'S GOT SOME WEIRD HISTORY WITH THIS CHAMMY GUY. I DON'T. I JUST FOUND HIM ON A TYPE OF CRAIGSLIST THAT ASSASSINS USE. IT'S CALLED CRAIGSLIST.

HAHA! ZING, CRAIGSLIST!

WHO IS SHE TALKING TO?

BEEP EEP

I AM GROOT?

<MUMBLY PHONE TALK BUT IT SOUNDS ANGRY>!!!

IS IT CAPTAIN MARVEL? TELL HER WE'RE DEALING WITH SOMETHING IMPORTANT. SKRULLS! NO, TOO OBVIOUS.

MOLE PEOPLE! TELL HER MOLE PEOPLE.

I AM GROOT.

<MORE MUMBLY PHONE TALK, IT SOUNDS CONFUSED>???

OH, RIGHT.

GIVE ME THE PHONE. I'LL TALK TO HER.

ALSO MY SWORD IS STILL STUCK IN THE TREE GUY. WHICH SUCKS 'CUZ IT'S A NICE SWORD. I THINK. ALL SWORDS SEEM PRETTY MUCH THE SAME.

ZING, SWORDS!

ROCKET! WHERE THE <CURSEWORD> ARE YOU GUYS?!

OH! HEY, CAROL!--PSSKHH--SAVING THE WORLD--PSHKKK--MOLE PEOPLE!--SKRR--PHHHS--PHONE BREAKING UP --SKRRR--

DIBS ON KICKING DOWN THE DOOR!

SETTLE DOWN. THERE'S NO NEED.

WHERE'S CHAMMY?!

WHO?

CHAMMY!

WHAP

WHERE'S CHAMMY?!

CHUNK

THA

I...I THINK YOU HAVE THE WRONG HOUSE. I DON'T KNOW ANYBODY NAMED CHAMMY.

MY BOYFRIEND'S NAME IS CHANDLER AND THERE'S NO WAY YOU'RE LOOKING FOR HIM.

CHANDLER! GET OUT OF THE BATHROOM AND MAKE THESE PEOPLE REPAIR OUR FRONT DOOR.

HE'S IN THE BATHROOM!

*Or whatever social media platform is popular when this goes to print.

NEARBY. AT SECRET COORDINATES.

H-HELLO? SMUGGLER GUY?

THANKS FOR DOING THIS.

ARE YOU COOL IF WE PICK UP MY GIRLFRIEND REAL QUICK?

I SHOULD WARN YOU, SHE'S GONNA YELL AT ME A BUNCH 'CAUSE SHE DOESN'T KNOW ANY OF THIS.

SO IF YOU'VE GOT EARS, I WOULD DO YOUR BEST TO PLUG 'EM.

SO, HOW'D YOU MEET GUS?

YOU DON'T TALK MUCH, HUH? SORRY. I END UP TALKING A LOT WHEN I'M NERVOUS.

TIK TIK TIK

BEEN A LONG TIME, CHAMMY.

Y'KNOW, YOU MUSTA BEEN GOOD AT HIDE-AND-SEEK. IT TOOK ME *FOREVER* TO FIND YOU.

LUCKY FOR ME, YOUR *FRIENDS* AREN'T AS GOOD AT HIDING AS YOU ARE.

SO, WE'VE GOT TWO OPTIONS HERE. OPTION ONE, YOU TELL ME WHAT I NEED TO KNOW, AND THEN I KILL YOU QUICK.

OR...OPTION TWO, YOU DON'T TELL ME AND I SUCK IT OUT OF YOUR HEAD REGARDLESS. BUT EVERY TIME I USE THAT POWER IT MAKES ME VOMIT. AND I *HATE* VOMITING.

WHICH IS WHY OPTION TWO WILL END WITH ME KILLING YOU...

REALLY.

REALLY.

SLOWLY.

YOU'RE GONNA TRY THE GUN AGAIN?! YOU KNOW WHAT? FINE. TAKE YOUR BEST SHOT.

SURE THING.

PSST! CHANDLER!

HUH?

RUTH?! WHAT ARE YOU DOING HERE?

SAVING YOUR LIFE.

AND THEN YELLING AT YOU.

LEMME TELL YOU WHY YOU'RE NOT GOING TO WIN THIS.

BECAUSE YOU'VE GOT THINGS TO LOSE.

BOOM

YOU'VE GOT FRIENDS AND FAMILY AND WANTS AND DESIRES AND PLANS.

SLAM

YOU'VE BEEN LYING TO ME FROM DAY ONE!!!

I'M SORRY. I HEAR Y--

APOLOGIZE ONE MORE TIME AND I WILL SHOVE THIS PINEAPPLE WHERE YOUR NOSE SHOULD BE!

I'M S-- OKAY.

SO WHAT WAS I? JUST PART OF YOUR COVER?!

SOME DUMB EARTH BIMBO TO HELP YOU KEEP UP APPEARANCES?

OF COURSE NOT!

THEN WHAT?! WHAT AM I TO YOU?!

YOU...

RUTH. THE PLAN WAS TO LIE LOW. FIND AN ISOLATED SPOT AND HIDE AWAY FROM THE UNIVERSE. ALONE.

FRESH FRUIT

"AND THEN I MET YOU."

"AND I FELL IN LOVE."

"BUT YOU FELL IN LOVE WITH *CHANDLER*."

AND I'M NOT CHANDLER. I'M CHAMMY. AND CHAMMY'S NOT A GOOD PERSON, RUTH. HE'S NOT A PERSON AT ALL.

...

I'M SORRY FOR DRAGGING YOU INTO THIS. I'LL MAKE SURE NO ONE BOTHERS Y--

YOU KNOW...

CHANDLER WAS BORING THE CRAP OUT OF ME.

david Lopez

SKREEEE

ALL RIGHT, EVERYBODY! QUICK AS YOU CAN!

GWEN! LET'S GO!

I'M NOT GOING.

COME ON! THAT LUNATIC'S GONNA KILL CAPTAIN MARVEL!

NO, HE'S NOT.

WHAT DO YOU MEAN, HE'S NOT?!

BECAUSE THEY'RE NOT GONNA KILL OFF CAPTAIN MARVEL IN A COMIC BOOK STARRING SQUIRREL AND THE TALKING TREE!

WHAT?

WHAT'S SHE TALKING ABOUT?

ALL RIGHT, LOOK. THERE'S LITERALLY *A WAR BETWEEN SUPER HEROES* GOING ON RIGHT NOW. AND WE'RE IN *GEORGIA* DOING STUFF THAT'S *COMPLETELY UNRELATED* TO ALL OF THAT. SO WHO DO YOU THINK'S WRITING THIS? IT'S PROBABLY SOME NOBODY WRITER WHO'S JUST STARTING OUT.

AND DO YOU HONESTLY THINK THEY'RE GONNA LET SOME SAD FREELANCER KILL OFF *CAPTAIN MARVEL?* ONE OF THEIR BIGGEST CHARACTERS?! YEAH, RIGHT.

IF ANYBODY'S GETTING KILLED OFF, IT'S GONNA BE ONE OF US. SORRY, BUT NO THANKS. I'M STAYING PUT.

I AM GROOT?

SORRY TO DESTROY THE DRAMATIC TENSION THERE, FOLKS, BUT YOU'VE GOTTA BE THINKING THE SAME THING.

THERE'S NO WAY THIS LOW-LEVEL WRITER HAS ANY AUTHORITY TO KILL A MAJOR SUPER HERO.

HOLY--

ARE YOU *KITTY PRYDE*?!

UH... YEAH.

WHAT ARE YOU DOING HERE?

I'M... ACTUALLY, I'M NOT TOTALLY SURE WHY I'M HERE.

OH @$#! IS %&@$ *BENDIS* WRITING THIS?

WHAT'S A BENDIS?

BENDIS. BRIAN MICHAEL BENDIS.

HE'S LIKE A BIG-DEAL COMIC BOOK WRITER.

HE USES TONS OF QUIPPY WORD BUBBLES AND PANELS AND I THINK HE HAS, LIKE, AN UNHEALTHY OBSESSION WITH YOU.

AND HE WOULD TOTALLY HAVE THE AUTHORITY TO KILL OFF CAPTAIN MARVEL!

SO, ARE YOU, LIKE, A CRAZY PERSON???

I NEED A TICKET FOR WHATEVER FLIGHT THE TREE AND SQUIRREL ARE ON! AND HURRY UP!

BRIAN MICHAEL BENDIS IS ABOUT TO KILL OFF CAPTAIN MARVEL!!

OKAY, I'VE GOT ONE TICKET LEFT, BUT IT'S A MIDDLE SEAT.

OH... YUCK.

HMM...IS THIS REALLY WORTH IT? I DON'T KNOW HER PERSONALLY...

I JUST DON'T SEE WHY YOU SHOULD GET THE AISLE, YOU HAVE THE SHORTEST LEGS OF ANY OF US!

THE TRISKELION.

GOOD WORK TODAY, GUYS. GET SOME REST.

WELL, AS MUCH AS I'D LIKE TO TAKE MY TIME WITH THIS, I DON'T WANT ANYONE TO SPOIL OUR--

HEY, REEVE. REMEMBER US?!

YOU TOOK US ON INDIVIDUALLY BEFORE, BUT NOW WE'RE WORKING AS A TEAM AND--

THAT'S RIGHT. WE'RE THE GWEN-DOW PANES.

NO, WE'RE NOT.

THE POINT IS, WE WORKED PAST OUR DIFFERENCES ON THE FLIGHT, AND NOW THAT WE'RE TOGETHER...

...WE'RE UNSTOPPABLE. SO--

AND YOU CAN CALL US GWEN AND THE-ART-OF-MOTORCYCLE-MAINTENANCES.

WILL YOU STOP?! THIS IS EXACTLY WHAT I WAS TALKING ABOUT.

THEN SETTLE ON A NAME! I'VE BEEN GIVING YOU GOLD, HERE!

WHAK

THAK

THUK

WOMP

LATER.

I WAS EXPERIMENTED ON ALONGSIDE REEVE. BUT THEY COULD ONLY GIVE ME ONE POWER...

WHERE'D HE GO?!

HOW'D HE ESCAPE?!

"...THE ABILITY TO MORPH INTO A PUDDLE OF WATER."

WHICH IS A PRETTY LAME SUPER-POWER. UNLESS NOBODY KNOWS ABOUT IT.

WELL, CHAMMY. THANK YOU. I OWE YOU MY LIFE.

ACTUALLY, WE'RE EVEN.

THE END.

AS THE HULK REPOSES ON THE ALIEN REDSWARD, TWO STRANGE FIGURES CONDUCT A CAUTIOUS EXAMINATION OF THE GREEN-SKINNED GOLIATH.

ALL I WANNA KNOW, WAL, IS-- IS HE ONE O' *JUDSON JAKES'* AUTOMATON ASSASSINS?

NEGATIVE, ROCKY! WHATEVER HE IS, HE'S ALIVE --

--AND BURSTING WITH AN INCREDIBLE CONCENTRATION OF GAMMA RADIATION!

THE PAIR ARE *ROCKET RACCOON*, GUARDIAN OF THE KEYSTONE QUADRANT...

...AND HIS FRIEND AND FIRST MATE, *WAL RUSS.*

SUDDENLY, ROCKET'S EARS DETECT A SUBTLE SOUND...

SNIKKERSNAK SNIKKERSNAK

WAL! A YOU-KNOW-WHAT'S COMIN'!

DO WE LEAVE THE GREEN ONE IN ITS PATH?

NO! SINCE HE'S ALIVE, WE GOTTA MOVE HIM! GIMME AN ϵUNGHH!ϵ PROSTHETIC!

WALDOES-- MECHANICAL ARMS-- SNAKE FROM WAL RUSS'S POUCH...

... BUT NOT EVEN *THEIR* POWER PROVES ENOUGH TO BUDGE A HALF-TON, SLEEPING HULK.

SNIKKERSNAK SNIKKERSNAK

WE AIN'T GETTIN' ANYWHERE, WAL!

AND THE YOU-KNOW-WHAT IS GETTING CLOSER, ROCKET!

SNIKKERSNAK SNIKKERSNAK

CORRECTION, WAL: *THE ROBOMOWER* IS *HERE!*

EGAD, ROCKET-- YOU'RE RIGHT!

2

WHERE *IS* HULK? WHO ARE FUNNY TALKING ANIMALS? WHAT IS GOING *ON*?!

THAT'S JUST WHAT WE WERE GOING TO ASK YOU, TALL, GREEN AND GRUESOME!

UH, ROCKET...

WAL, CAN'T YOU SEE THAT I'M DEEPLY ENGROSSED IN CONVERSATION WITH OUR GREEN GUEST?

WELL, GET *UN*ENGROSSED! I JUST GOT A TINGLE ON MY *FUZZ-DETECTOR!*

PING-A-LING

FUZZ² WHAT ARE "FUZZ?"

BULLS, HULK! JOHN-LAW! POLICE! THE *COPS!*

THE ROBO-MOWER MUST HAVE GOTTEN OFF AN ALARM!

HULK IS NOT AFRAID OF POLICE!

NEITHER ARE *WE*, HULK...

STOP----IN THE NAME OF THE LAW!

THAT'S US!

LOOK OUT!

"...IT'S JUST THAT WE HAVE MUCH TO DO, AND LITTLE TIME TO WASTE WHEN IT COMES TO *THE KEYSTONE QUADRANT KOPS!*"

WE'VE JUST RUN OVER THE VICTIM!

BOOK HIM!

HE'S INTERFERING WITH THE COURSE OF JUSTICE!

HE'S NOT A *HIM*-- HE'S AN *IT!*

THOSE ARE... *POLICE??!*

WELL, LOOSELY SPEAKING, THEIR PURPOSE IS TO PRESERVE LAW AND DISORDER!

WHICH THEY DO TO IMPERFECTION!

SUMMON OUR SHIP, WAL!

YOUR SHIP!

LOOK, JUST BECAUSE *I* MADE THE PAYMENTS DOESN'T MEAN WE CAN'T CO-OWN THE BLASTED SHIP!

IS THAT WHY IT'S CALLED *RAKK'N'RUIN* AND NOT THE *WAILING WAL?*

5

I CAN'T HELP IT IF **RAKK** AND **ROCKET** ARE ALLITERATIVE! I DIDN'T NAME THE SHIP--**LYLLA** DID!

SHE'S **YOUR** GIRLFRIEND!

GEEPS! SHE'S **YOUR** NIECE!

WHAT ARE TALKING ANIMALS ARGUING ABOUT?

OH, VARIOUS SUNDRIES--

--WHILE **I** PREPARE TO LAUNCH **HIS** SHIP!

VROAR

BLAST-OFF!

ROBO-SLAUGHTER-ERS!

SOMEBODY GET THEIR LICENSE NUMBER!

MOWER-MURDERERS!

TRAFFIC-VIOLATERS!

DESPITE THE KEYSTONE QUADRANT KOPS' PROTESTATIONS, THE **RAKK-'N'RUIN** TAKES TO THE SKY.

WELL, HULK, YOU MUST BE HUNGRY AND CONFUSED--

FOOD 'N' STUFF

--SO ALLOW ME TO FEED YOU BEFORE I WELCOME YOU ABOARD THE TRUSTY **RAKK'N'RUIN!**

PTUI!

DINNER IS SERVED, MASTER ROCKET!

THANKS, SHIP!

SOON...

FOOD IS ALMOST GONE, BUT HULK STILL DOESN'T KNOW WHERE HULK IS, OR HOW HULK GOT HERE!

WE CAN'T HELP YOU WITH THE SECOND, HULK, YOU SEEMED TO APPEAR OUT OF NOWHERE!

BUT PART ONE IS EASY: WE FOUND YOU ON **HALF-WORLD**, HULK--

"--LARGEST PLANET IN THE STAR SYSTEM KNOWN AS THE **KEYSTONE QUADRANT!**"

IMAGES FLASH ON THE MONITOR-SCREENS OF THE RAKK'N'RUIN.

VERY STRANGE IMAGES!

6

HUNH! HULK HAS NEVER SEEN WORLD WITH A WALL AROUND IT BEFORE!

THE *GALACIAN WALL* SURROUNDS THE ENTIRE KEYSTONE QUADRANT, HULK. IT'S INCREDIBLY ANCIENT--NO ONE KNOWS WHO BUILT IT.

WE ONLY KNOW *WHY:* IT'S PURPOSE IS TO KEEP EVERYONE IN THE QUADRANT *IN*--AND EVERYONE OUTSIDE THE QUADRANT *OUT!*

HULK GOT IN!

YEAH, YOU DID! ANY IDEA HOW?

ALL HULK REMEMBERS IS BEING INSIDE *GALAXY MASTER*,* AND THEN WAKING UP ON RED GRASS!

*LAST ISH--AL.

RIGHT! NOW, AS I WAS SAYING--

"... THE WALL ENCIRCLES THE WHOLE QUADRANT! *HALF-WORLD*-- WHERE YOU WOKE UP-- IS WHERE WAL AND I HAIL FROM!

"WHY'S IT CALLED *HALFWORLD,* YOU ASK?

"BECAUSE *HALF* OF IT IS STRIPPED BARE-- AN INDUSTRIAL WASTELAND WHERE AUTOMATONS LABOR AS THEY'VE LABORED FOREVER ON A GIANT HUMANOID SPACECRAFT KNOWN ONLY AS *SHIP!*

"THE *OTHER* HALF IS A PARADISE PLANET WHERE WE ANIMALS PLAY AND FARM WITH MACHINES THE AUTOMATONS GIVE US...

"...'CAUSE THEY CAN'T HELP MAKIN' EM, AND CAN'T USE 'EM ONCE THEY DO!

ARE THERE NO PUNY HUMANS ON PLANET?

ONLY THE *KEYSTONE KOPS*, HULK-- 'HUMAN' IS A WORD I'VE HEARD THEM CALL THEM- SELVES. I ALWAYS ASSUMED IT SIGNIFIED SOME DERANGED SPECIES OF ANIMAL.

IF THERE ARE POLICE, THERE MUST BE TROUBLE!

YOU CAN BET YOUR EMERALD EYES THERE'S TROU- BLE IN THE QUADRANT, HULK!

7

"AND IT ALL STEMS FROM A MURDEROUS MOLE NAME OF *JUDSON JAKES*! NO ONE KNOWS WHAT HE'S UP TO, EXCEPT THAT HE SITS IN THE CENTER OF THE KEYSTONE QUADRANT ABOARD HIS *SPACEWHEEL* LIKE A FAT SPIDER IN THE MIDDLE OF A WEB!

"JAKES HEADS A COMPANY CALLED *INTER-STEL MECHANICS* WHOSE CHIEF SCIENTIST, A TORTOISE NAME OF *UNCLE PYKO*, TURNS OUT *AUTOMATON ASSASSINS* LIKE THE *KILLER CLOWNS* AN' THE DREAD *DRAKILLARS*, AN' HIRES RENEGADE RABBITS, LIKE *THE BLACK BUNNY BRIGADE*, TO DO HIS DIRTY WORK!"

SO? SO JAKES IS MAKIN' ALL THESE MACHINE-MARAUDERS FOR ONE PURPOSE ONLY, HULK! HE WANTS TO GET HIS PAWS ON THE GREATEST TREASURE IN THE KEYSTONE QUADRANT!

A BOOK CALLED *GIDEON'S BIBLE!*

WRITTEN BY THE *FIRSTCOMERS*, IT'S SUPPOSED TO HOLD THE SECRET ORIGIN OF THE KEYSTONE QUADRANT AND ITS INHABITANTS ON ITS PAGES!

BUT IT IS WRITTEN IN A LANGUAGE WHICH NO ONE CAN READ.

UH, ROCKET...

...WE'RE GETTING AN *EMERGENCY ALERT* FROM *LYLLA!*

THERE'S HAVOC ON HALFWORLD!

A TERRIBLE IMAGE FILLS THE MONITOR-SCREEN.

CUCKOO'S NEST TO *RAKK'N'RUIN*-- THE *BLACK BUNNY BRIGADE* HAS LAUNCHED AN ATTACK!

WHAT IS... CUCKOO'S NEST?

THAT'S WHERE GIDEON'S BIBLE IS KEPT, HULK!

WE NEVER THOUGHT JUDSON JAKES WOULD DARE ATTACK OUR STRONGHOLD!

WELL HE HAS--AND IF HE SEIZES GIDEON'S BIBLE AND GETS UNCLE PYKO TO DECIPHER IT, THERE'S NO TELLING WHAT TERRIBLE SECRETS HE'LL LEARN, WHAT AWFUL FATE HE'LL UNLEASH ON THE KEYSTONE QUADRANT!

TO STOP HIM, WE'LL HAVE TO GO UP AGAINST JAKES HIMSELF!

HULK-- WILL YOU HELP US?!

HULK IS HERE BECAUSE HE HELPED SOMEONE ELSE!

HULK HAD TO LEAVE HIS FRIENDS BACK ON *EARTH!*

RICK AND BETTY WILL WORRY ABOUT HULK! HULK SHOULD GET HOME! BUT HULK'S HEAD FEELS SO STRANGE, HULK DOESN'T KNOW *WHAT* TO DO!

8

WHY OUR JADE GIANT FEELS STRANGE IS A TOPIC WE'LL DELVE INTO *NEXT MONTH*.

MEANWHILE, LET US CAST OUR GAZE BRIEFLY EARTHWARD...

...TO A FORSAKEN STRETCH OF DESERT WHERE, YEARS BEFORE, IN A BLAZE OF GAMMA-GREEN FIRE, THE *HULK* WAS BORN.

THE ONLY FIRE NOW COMES FROM THE SUN.

BUT NOT EVEN THE SUN'S RAYS CAN PENETRATE THE DARK FASTNESS OF THE CAVE COMPLEX BENEATH THE DESERT SANDS...

...WHERE, UNTIL RECENTLY, *DR. BRUCE BANNER* LABORED TO KILL OR CURE HIS EMERALD ALTER-EGO.

THEN CAME THE *HULK-HUNTERS* SEEKING THE HULK'S HELP AGAINST THE RAVAGES OF THE *GALAXY MASTER* AND HIS SAVAGE SERVANT, THE *ABOMINATION!* BANNER BECAME THE HULK, FOUGHT THE HULK-HUNTERS, AND THEN ACCOMPANIED THEM ON A QUEST TO THE FAR REACHES OF THE COSMOS. *

HE HAD NO WAY OF KNOWING THAT, IN HIS WAKE, RICK JONES HAD SUBJECTED HIMSELF TO A DEADLY DOSE OF GAMMA RAYS IN A MAD ATTEMPT TO MAKE OF HIMSELF A SECOND HULK!

RICK ALMOST DIED. THAT LEFT BETTY ROSS ALONE TO DEAL WITH THE DESPERATE NEED TO GET RICK TO A HOSPITAL...

...AND THE COMING OF THE KRYLORIAN BIRD-WOMAN, *BEREET!*

WH-WHAT IN HEAVEN'S NAME *ARE* YOU ?!?

I HAVE ALREADY TOLD YOU, I AM *BEREET*, TECHNO-ARTIST FROM THE PLANET KRYLOR. I HAVE COME TO MAKE A DOCUMENTARY ABOUT THE INCREDIBLE HULK!

GREEPLE REEP?

A PITY IT MUST BEGIN WITH THE DEATH-SCENE OF THE HULK'S CLOSEST FRIEND!

HUSH, STURKY-- THIS IS A SOMBER MOMENT!

WE MUST OBSERVE THE PROPER SOLEMNITIES, AND THEN BEGIN FILMING.

9

GIVEN WHAT SHE HAS GONE THROUGH IN THE PAST FEW HOURS, BEREET'S ANNOUNCEMENT IS MORE THAN BETTY CAN BEAR.

Y-YOU'RE NOT GOING TO HELP ME *SAVE* RICK?!

YOU'RE GOING TO STAND BY AND WATCH HIM DIE?!

YOU'RE GOING TO MAKE A MOVIE OF IT??!

REEP!

YES, STURKY-- SHE IS DISTRAUGHT. CALM HER.

REEP

GREEPLE

SPOK

ALL RIGHT, I'M IN CONTROL AGAIN. NOW YOU LISTEN...

RICK JONES HAS SUBJECTED HIMSELF TO A MASSIVE DOSAGE OF GAMMA RADIATION -- THE SAME RADIATION THAT TURNED BRUCE BANNER INTO THE HULK. ALL IT'S DONE TO RICK IS NEARLY KILL HIM.

HE NEEDS TO GET TO A DOCTOR.

AND YOU WANT MY HELP? OH, MY...

...THAT DOES COMPLICATE THINGS, YOU SEE, I'M HERE TO FILM A DOCUMENTARY.

KRYLORIAN ENTERTAINMENT CODE XV-III EXPRESSLY FORBIDS TECHNO-ARTISTS FROM INTERFERING IN THE COURSE OF THEIR NON-FICTION FILMS.

HOWEVER, KRYLORIAN TECHNO-ARTISTS ARE KNOWN FOR IGNORING ENTERTAINMENT CODE XV-III

BEREET REACHES INTO THE BAG AT HER HIP...

...AND OUT COMES A SPIDERY SOMETHING THAT GROWS IN SIZE UNTIL IT ALL BUT ENCOMPASSES THE UNCONSCIOUS RICK.

THE **LIFE SUPPORT SPIDER** WILL STABILIZE RICK'S CONDITION. HE WILL GROW NO BETTER, BUT HE WILL ALSO GROW NO WORSE.

YOU SAID YOU **KNEW** RICK AND THE HULK, HOW?

MANY YEARS AGO I MADE A FILM WITH THEM. IT WAS HAILED AS A MASTER-PIECE ON KRYLOR.*

*IT WAS ALSO THE SUBJECT OF **RAMPAGING HULK** #1-9--ARCHIVAL AL.

AT THAT POINT, RICK RE-VIVES AND WHISPERS...

B-BETTY... NEVER SAW... THIS GEEK... IN MY LIFE.

...AND THEN LAPSES INTO UNCONSCIOUSNESS AGAIN.

NEEDLESS TO SAY, HIS WORDS ARE THE **LAST** THING BETTY ROSS NEEDS TO HEAR.

WELL, STURKY, THIS DOES POSE A PROBLEM.

REEP

MEANWHILE, BACK IN THE KEYSTONE QUADRANT...

...WE'VE COME HALFWAY 'ROUND HALFWORLD, HULK--

--AND THERE'S **CUCKOO'S NEST** DEAD-AHEAD!

THE MOUND-COMPOUND IS SINISTERLY SILENT. UNCONSCIOUS ANIMALS LIE STREWN ABOUT.

WHAT HAS HAPPENED HERE?

THE WORST, HULK!

THE **BLACK BUNNY BRIGADE!**

ROCKY, **STINKER** SEEKS TO SPEAK!

STINKER, OLD PAL! WE CAME AS SOON AS WE COULD! WHERE'S **LYLLA?**

T-TAKEN, ROCKY...

...ALONG WITH... **GIDEON'S BIBLE!**

TAKEN? WHERE?!

ONLY ONE PLACE, WAL-- TO **SPACE-WHEEL...** AND TO **JUDSON JAKES!**

MURDER DARKENS ROCKET RACCOON'S EYES.

11

SPACEWHEEL!

ROUND AND ROUND AND ROUND IT GOES...

...AND WHERE IT STOPS, ONLY *JUDSON JAKES* KNOWS!

I MUST REMEMBER TO HAVE UNCLE PYKO STABI-LIZE SPACEWHEEL'S SPIN. APPARENTLY, THE ENTIRE CREW IS SUFFERING FROM VERTIGO.

I'LL GET RIGHT ON IT-- JUST AS SOON AS I DECIPHER THIS INDECIPHERABLE TOME YOU HAD YOUR HENCH-RABBIT HIJACK!

QUIT COMPLAININ', PYKO! YOU GOT A CUSH DESK JOB UP HERE ON SPACEWHEEL, WHILE *BLACKJACK O'HARE* AND HIS *BLACK BUNNY BRIGADE* DO ALL THE DIRTY WORK!

PRESENT COMPANY EXCEPTED, LYLLA, DARLIN'!

UNHAND ME, YOU WRETCHED RABBIT! WHEN MY ROCKY GETS HERE--!

HE WILL RECEIVE THE WARMEST OF WELCOMES, MY DEAR!

AND COME HE WILL, FOR HE IS THE SWORN GUARDIAN OF *GIDEON'S BIBLE*...

...THE BOOK WHOSE SECRETS WILL MAKE ME MASTER OF THE KEYSTONE QUADRANT!

YOU MEAN THE BOOK THAT'S GOING TO GIVE ME AND MY COMPUTERS EYESTRAIN? THIS THING DON'T MAKE SENSE!

FUNNY LETTERS! INCOMPREHENSIBLE ALPHABET! A GOBBLEDYGOOK OF GRAMMATICAL ERRORS! WHAT KIND OF LAN-GUAGE DID THE FIRSTCOMERS SPEAK?

THAT IS PRECISELY WHAT I EXPECT YOU TO *DIS-COVER*, PYKO.

AND, PLEASE, YOUR FEIGNED IGNORANCE INSULTS MY INTELLIGENCE. YOU ARE A GENIUS, UNCLE, IT WAS YOU WHO BUILT SPACE-WHEEL.

IF YA ASK ME, HE KNOWS MORE'N IS GOOD FOR HIM!

OH! WHAT'S THAT HORRIBLE CREATURE?!

JUST A *DRA-KILLAR*, MY DEAR-- ONE OF THE COUNTLESS SENTRIES I HAVE POSTED THROUGH-OUT THE QUADRANT.

IT IS TELE-PATHICALLY TELLING ME THAT YOUR BOYFRIEND HAS ARRIVED!

12

HOW FORTUNATE ROCKET CHOSE TO DROP IN TODAY! WE'VE A SPECIAL TREAT FOR HIM, HAVEN'T WE, PYKO?

THE *CIRCUS* IS IN TOWN!

DO SEND IN THE *CLOWNS*, UNCLE, ON YOUR WAY BACK TO YOUR LABORATORY!

THAT OLD SNAIL-SLOW SCIENTIST? WHY DON'TCHA LET ME COOK HIM IN HIS SHELL, BOSS?

CAN *YOU* DECIPHER *GIDEON'S BIBLE*, RABBIT?

UH, I ONCE SKIMMED A PAMPHLET ON TORTURE TECHNIQUES!

OH, ROCKET-- PLEASE BE CAREFUL!

DELIGHTFUL BEDTIME READING, I WAGER!

CAUTIOUSLY, THE *RAKK'N'RUIN* DRAWS NEAR THE SPINNING *SPACEWHEEL*.

THERE SHE BLOWS, WAL--JUDSON JAKES'S *MURDER-GO-ROUND!*

I KNOW. I PILOTED US HERE.

SO WHAT DO YOU WANT --A MEDAL? I'M THE ONE WHO'S GOTTA BLAST IN AN' GET LYLLA OUT!

HULK HAS MADE UP HIS MIND. HULK WILL HELP.

I'M GLAD TO HEAR THAT, SPINACH- SKIN--

"--'CAUSE HERE COMES THE WELCOME WAGON! UNCLE PYKO'S *KILLER CLOWNS!*"

CYBORG ASSASSINS, THEY SKIP ACROSS SPACE ON SILENT ROCKET-SKATES, THEIR GAY GARB BETOKENING NOT MERRIMENT...

13

...BUT *MURDER!*

DESPITE ITS DEFENSE-SCREENS, THE RAKK'N'RUIN IS SHOCKED, RATTLED AND ROLLED!

HULK WANTS TO GO OUT AND SMASH STUPID CLOWNS!

THIS IS NO LAUGHING MATTER!

I DON'T THINK WE'VE GOT A SPACESUIT THAT WOULD FIT YOU, HULK!

NO, BUT WE'VE GOT A JUMBO-SIZED HELMET!

I'M BETTING THE HULK'S SKIN IS TOUGH ENOUGH TO WITHSTAND THE COLD OF SPACE.

WAIT, HULK! LET ME TURN ON YOUR *INTER-COMMUNICATOR!*

HULK SAID, HULK IS NOT AFRAID OF SPACE!

THAT'S GOOD, GREEN-GUY--'CAUSE INTO *SPACE* IS WHERE WE'RE GOING, TO KAYO THOSE *KILLER CLOWNS!*

...AND NOW, IN CENTER RING, ROCKET RACCOON...

14

THE HULK'S CRY OF WARNING COMES A TAD TOO LATE, FOR THE *LEADER* OF THE *KILLER CLOWNS* IS ALREADY UPON OUR RIGHTEOUS RACCOON!

A GREAT PRIZE AWAITS THE ONE WHO SLAYS YOU, RODENT!

THE PRIZE OF *LIFE* -- TO CEASE BEING A COLD CYBORG KILLING MACHINE...

...AND BECOME INSTEAD A *LIVING BEING!*

A LIFE FOR A *DEATH,* CLOWN? CUTE TRADE!

GEEPS! *LASER CONTACT-LENSES* TRYING TO OPEN MY HELMET! *HELP!!*

HELP IS AT HAND...

RAARRHH!

HULK! THANKS A LOT!

DID ROCKET THINK THAT HULK WOULD LET CLOWN KILL HIM?

TO TELL YOU THE TRUTH, GREENSKIN, RATIONAL THOUGHT GAVE WAY TO PANIC AS THOSE LASERS STARTED TO SIZZLE MY HELMET! THIS IS ONE RACCOON WHO LIKES *BREATHING!*

CLOWNS ARE ALL GONE! NOW WHAT DO HULK AND ROCKET DO?

THE JOB WE CAME FOR, SPINACH-SKIN!

WE ENTER *SPACEWHEEL* TO SAVE *LYLLA* AND *GIDEON'S BIBLE...* AND WE DON'T COME BACK WITHOUT 'EM!

QUESTION IS: *HOW DO WE GET IN??!*

16

LEAVE THAT TO *HULK!*

PUHWRAKK!

CERTAINLY! ANY TIME!

NOW THAT WE'RE IN, WHERE DO WE FIND ROCKET'S GIRLFRIEND AND MYSTERY BOOK?

BEATS ME! I'VE ALWAYS BEEN SORT OF *FERA NON GRATA* ABOARD SPACEWHEEL!

GUESS WE'LL JUST HAVE TO PEEK IN DOORS!

THERE'S LAWS AGAINST *PEEPIN' TOMS,* RODENT!

THERE--WITH LYLLA! IT'S *BLACKJACK O'HARE!*

WHO--?

LEADER OF THE *BLACK BUNNY BRIGADE!*

RIGHT! YOU CAN TAKE OFF YOUR FISHBOWL, ROCKET-- PYKO'S *SERVODROIDS* HAVE ALREADY REPAIRED THE HOLE YOUR FRIEND PUNCHED IN SPACEWHEEL!

NOW, SURRENDER, OR THERE'LL BE OTTER BRAINS ALL OVER THE BULKHEAD!

I...YOU DON'T LEAVE ME MUCH CHOICE, RABBIT!

MUCH CHOICE? RACCOON, I DON'T LEAVE YOU *ANY* CHOICE!

I'M NOT FOOL ENOUGH TO TAKE CHANCES WITH THE *FASTEST GUN* IN THE KEYSTONE QUADRANT!

RUN, ROCKET! *RUN!*

SURE! RUN! I DON'T MIND SHOOTIN' YA IN THE BACK!

NO! RABBIT WILL NOT SHOOT ANYBODY!

HULK, DON'T! HE'LL KILL LYLLA! THERE'S NO WAY WE CAN REACH HIM FROM HERE--!

HULK DOES NOT HAVE TO *REACH* RABBIT TO *STOP* HIM!

WHOM!

17

SEE?

YOIKS!

KEEP IN MIND, BLACKJACK: NOBODY KNOWS YOU WHEN YOU'RE DOWN:

...AND *OUT!*

SPOK!

OH, ROCKY-- I DO WISH YOU WOULD TAKE OFF THAT SILLY HELMET SO I COULD KISS YOU!

LATER, LYLLA! WE STILL HAVE TO RETRIEVE GIDEON'S BIBLE AND GET BACK TO THE RAKK-'N'RUIN!

FOLLOW US, HULK!

THE HULK STARTS TO FOLLOW...

...BUT HALFWAY DOWN THE CORRIDOR A FAMILIAR GREEN GLOW CATCHES HIS EMERALD EYE.

COME IN, MY FRIEND! I'VE BEEN WAITING FOR YOU!

HUNH?

YOU ARE... TURTLE?!

INDUBITABLY, PYKO'S THE NAME... *UNCLE PYKO.* BY THE WAY: RECOGNIZE THE PLANET ON MY VIEWSCREEN?

HOME! HULK'S HOME!!

AH, RIGHT AGAIN! I THOUGHT I MIGHT BE!

BUT THEN, I'M RIGHT ABOUT EVERYTHING --AS MY EMPLOYER JUDSON JAKES, WILL ONE DAY LEARN TO HIS INFINITE SORROW.

BUT THAT DOESN'T CONCERN YOU, DOES IT? NO, YOU JUST WANT TO GO HOME --TO *EARTH!* WELL, I CAN ARRANGE IT, TO THE MUTUAL ADVANTAGE OF US BOTH!

18

AS OUR GREEN-SKINNED GOLIATH STRUGGLES TO UNDERSTAND THE PUZZLING PYKO, ROCKET RACCOON AND LYLLA FIND THE LAIR OF...

JUDSON JAKES!

BEYOND A DOUBT. A MOST GRACIOUS WELCOME, FRIEND ROCKET, TO MY HUMBLE ABODE.

CUT THE COMEDY, MOLE--AND HAND OVER THE BOOK!

BOOK? WHICH BOOK? I HAVE SO MANY--

--AND SO LITTLE TIME TO READ WITH ALL THESE INTERRUPTIONS! *DRAKILLAR!* BID MY UNINVITED GUESTS DEPART...

...THAT I MIGHT CONTINUE MY MEDITATIONS.

ROCKY, LOOK *OUT!*

19   IT'S A DRAKILLAR!

A *NEW-BEAST*--CREATED IN OLD UNCLE PYKO'S LAB!

MUST'VE BEEN A HARMLESS LITTLE BAT ONCE--

VREET

--CURSE UNCLE PYKO!

AND CURSE *YOU*, MOLE, FOR MAKING ME SHOOT DOWN SOMETHING THAT WAS ONCE ONE OF OUR OWN KIND!

YOUR KIND, YOU MEAN, RACCOON! I AM *JUDSON JAKES*--I AM BEYOND THE MERE ANIMAL EXISTENCE WHICH YOU SO ARDENTLY PROTECT!

YEAH? *SO FAR* BEYOND IT THAT YOU'LL THREATEN IT ALL WITH WHATEVER SECRETS YOU FIND IN *GIDEON'S BIBLE*, HUH?

THE BOOK, MOLE! I WANT IT NOW-- OR ELSE YOU'RE GONNA BECOME SEVERELY *DECOMPRESSED!*

NO! DON'T DAMAGE SPACEWHEEL!

I'LL SUMMON PYKO!

AND, IN UNCLE PYKO'S LABORATORY...

BRRZZZT

AH, THE MASTER OF SPACEWHEEL SUMMONS! HE MUST HAVE AC-KNOWLEDGED DEFEAT, AS I KNEW HE WOULD!

I KNOW SO MANY THINGS I SHOULDN'T KNOW, HULK--SUCH AS WHO YOU ARE, WHERE YOU CAME FROM, ETCETERA.

PLANET ON SCREEN IS *EARTH*, HULK'S HOME.

THAT IS WHERE HULK'S FRIENDS-- *RICK* AND *BETTY*-- WAIT FOR HULK!

CAN TALKING TURTLE SEND HULK HOME?

OF COURSE! THE *GALACIAN WALL* SURROUNDING THE *KEYSTONE QUADRANT* PREVENTS ITS INHABITANTS FROM EVER LEAVING THIS MADHOUSE UNIVERSE --

-- BUT NO BARRIER IS INSUPERABLE TO ONE WHO HAS FATHOMED THE SECRETS OF THE *FIRST-COMERS*, TO ONE WHO COMPREHENDS THE MYSTERIES OF *GIDEON'S BIBLE!*

HULK THOUGHT THAT NO ONE COULD READ MYSTERY BOOK.

NO ONE BUT ME, HULK, AND EVEN *I* DISCOVERED HOW QUITE BY ACCIDENT...

...FROM DEEPLY-SUBMERGED MEMORIES WHICH I DREDGED FORTH ONE DAY WHEN I WAS PROBING THE ADDLED BRAIN OF A *KEYSTONE COP*, POOR CREATURE! HE DIDN'T SURVIVE THE PROBE!

IT SEEMS THAT THOSE LOONY-TUNE COPS ARE DIRECTLY DESCENDED FROM THE *FIRST-COMERS*--

--AS ARE *YOU*, HULK! THAT'S HOW I DEDUCED WHERE YOU CAME FROM AND HOW TO SEND YOU BACK!

20

AND YOU *MUST* GO HOME, HULK! THERE'S A BALANCE OF POWER HERE IN THE KEYSTONE QUADRANT BETWEEN MY TECHNOLOGY--

--AND ROCKET RACCOON AND THE OTHER ANIMALS, YOUR MIGHT WOULD TIP THE SCALES IN THEIR FAVOR. I CAN'T ALLOW THAT, SO I'M SENDING YOU HOME.

ALL HULK KNOWS IS THAT HULK DOESN'T BELONG HERE! SEND HULK HOME, TALKING TURTLE!

A SWITCH IS THROWN...

...WHILE, AT THE HUB OF SPACEWHEEL, ROCKET RACCOON'S FINGER GROWS ITCHY ON HIS TRIGGER.

I'M RUNNING OUT OF PATIENCE, JAKES! LYLLA'S GOT A HELMET ON NOW, SO THERE'S NOTHING STOPPING ME FROM BLASTING A HOLE IN YOUR PICTURE WINDOW...!

PLEASE, ROCKET --THAT'S THE BEST VIEW ON SPACEWHEEL!

ROCKY, IT'S THE TURTLE!

PYKO!

THE BOOK, UNCLE-- GIVE HIM THE BOOK!!

GIDEON'S BIBLE? WHY, CERTAINLY! IMPENETRABLE PROSE, YOU KNOW. COULDN'T MAKE HEAD NOR TAILS OF IT!

I'M AFRAID IT WILL NEVER BE A BEST-SELLER!

GIDEON'S BIBLE

MAYBE NOT, BUT AT LEAST IT'LL BE SAFE WHERE IT BELONGS BACK IN IT'S SHRINE AT CUCKOO'S NEST!

AN APPROPRIATE NAME, IF I DO SAY SO MYSELF!

WHY? NOBODY KNOWS WHAT CUCKOO'S NEST MEANS!

OF COURSE NOT! I'D FORGOTTEN! OH, LOOK! THERE GOES YOUR FRIEND!

MY FRIEND--?

YES! THE HULK, I BELIEVE HE WAS CALLED!

HULK!

THE FLASHING GREEN BEAM TRAVERSING SPACE DOES NOT ACKNOWLEDGE ROCKET RACCOON'S CALL...

...AND, IN AN INSTANT, THE BEAM IS LOST TO SIGHT.

HE'S GONE--OUT OF THE KEYSTONE QUADRANT! BUT, HOW?!

I SUSPECT WHAT-EVER BROUGHT HIM HERE... WORE OFF!

YOU KNOW MORE THAN YOU'RE TEL-LING, TURTLE!

ALWAYS, BUT YOU HAVE YOUR BOOK, AND YOUR SHIP IS WAITING!

21

THEN, WHEN ROCKET AND LYLLA HAVE DISEMBARKED FROM SPACEWHEEL...

BLAST! WE FINALLY HAD GIDEON'S BIBLE IN OUR HANDS!

IT WOULDN'T HAVE DONE YOU ANY GOOD -- NOT EVEN MY COMPUTERS COULD READ IT!

IT WAS ALL GREEK TO THEM!

GREEK? WHAT'S "GREEK?"

A SYNONYM FOR INCOMPREHENSIBLE, IF YOU ASK ME. I DON'T THINK GIDEON'S BIBLE MAKES ANY SENSE AT ALL!

WHAT ABOUT THAT GREEN CREATURE WHO AIDED THE RACCOON?

THE HULK? I IMAGINE HE'S ON HIS WAY... HOME!

ON THE BRIDGE OF THE RAKK-'N'-RUIN...

SORRY, ROCKET-- I DETECT NO GAMMA TRACE OF THE HULK ANYWHERE...

I WISH I KNEW WHAT HAPPENED TO HIM! WE OWE SPINACH-SKIN A LOT!

WELL, MAYBE OUR PATHS WILL CROSS AGAIN--

--SOMEDAY!

PERHAPS, BUT IN THE INTERIM THE STAGE IS NOW SET FOR WHAT PROMISES TO BE THE MOST STARTLING SERIES OF CHANGES IN THE LIFE OF THE INCREDIBLE HULK YET!

CANCEL WHATEVER OTHER APPOINTMENTS YOU MAY HAVE MADE AND BE HERE FOR THE INCREDIBLE HULK #272, ENTITLED...

"...I HAVE A BRAIN, BUT I MUST SCREAM!"

22